Listening to the Corn

To: Jeanne

Best wishes always,

[signature]

Listening to the Corn

Poetry of Gerard A. Geiger

iUniverse, Inc.
New York Lincoln Shanghai

Listening to the Corn

All Rights Reserved © 2003 by Gerard Andrew Geiger

No part of this book may be reproduced or transmitted in any form or by any means, graphic, electronic, or mechanical, including photocopying, recording, taping, or by any information storage retrieval system, without the written permission of the publisher.

iUniverse, Inc.

For information address:
iUniverse, Inc.
2021 Pine Lake Road, Suite 100
Lincoln, NE 68512
www.iuniverse.com

ISBN: 0-595-27506-0

Printed in the United States of America

Dedication: To my wife, Cindy, my source of strength and inspiration; and to my children, Rachel, Hillary, and Shawn, who are my most sincere critics and ardent supporters.

Contents

Remember You are Jerseymen 1
    (Civil War Monument Statue, Hackettstown, N.J.)
Soft Iron 3
On Writing Poetry 5
Effects 6
Autumnal Protest 7
Mind Traveler 9
Closure 11
Chance of Love 12
Winter Woods 13
Honour 15
View of a Field in February 17
Generation of a Stream 18
Heron 21
I Dream of Dancing in the Streets 23
Barefoot 27
Sideshow 28
Listening to the Corn 30
Mill Pond Falls 32
    (Old Red Mill, Clinton, N.J.)
Oak in the Woods 35
Structure 37

Why does a Poet write?	*39*
Bison (Ode to the American Buffalo)	*41*
Thaw	*43*
Chat with Dr. Hereford	*45*
The Grain Field	*47*
Disinherited	*49*
Hunting	*52*
Mother Corn	*54*
Social Physics	*56*
Interlude	*58*
Sentinel	*60*
Autumn Wind	*62*
Raptor	*63*
Birch 101	*65*
Flutterspeed	*66*
October at Oxford Lake	*68*
Herald of Winter	*70*
Without Love	*72*
Imponderable	*74*
Dissonance	*76*
Germination	*78*
Spring House	*80*
Country Graveyard	*82*
Rat Jack	*84*
Economics of the Street	*85*
Fool for Love	*87*
Flip-Flop	*89*
Cold Creek and Ice	*91*

Gerard A. Geiger

He is… *93*
Author Biography *95*

Introduction: Listening to the Corn is my second book of poems, a collection of forty six I have written since March 2000, plus reprints of three selected because of their common themes. I feel this volume of poetry is more personal in that it delves into my inner thoughts while I observe the natural world around me.

Many of these poems were composed while I was taking my daily two mile constitutional in the country along the roads and fields of the farmland bordering my home in Warren County, New Jersey. Others in this collection refer to specific themes explained in an accompanying note. All of these poems are a part of me which I share unabashedly with you, my reader, in the spirit of openness and friendship. Thank you in advance for your patient ear, and I look forward to taking more poetic walks with you in the future.

Gerard

March 20, 2003 Port Murray, N.J. 07865

Remember You are Jerseymen

I stand before you calm and serene,
my expression belies the horrors I've seen.

My coat of blue, now in bronze bereaved;
a patina of age I never achieved.

We find in life tempests to brave,
swords to clash and ideals to save.

I saw my duty to follow such light,
no matter the fury or how dark the night.

I stand as a guidon for Jerseymen fair,
protecting our Union from threats we share.

Though I stand a statue, a Jerseyman blue,
I was once a young man made of flesh like you.

No more verdant hills or streams will I roam,
to you I bequeath this land as your home.

Protect her and the children from tyrants and fools
and "Remember you are Jerseymen" where freedom rules.

Gerard A. Geiger   May 22, 2000

This poem is inscribed on the side of the new Civil War Memorial erected and rededicated in Hackettstown, N.J. on Memorial Day, 2001. Picture of original statue on following page.

Listening to the Corn

Gerard A. Geiger

Soft Iron

It's mined from every community
in every city and town.
It's in every organization
where the needs of men are found.

It's the elemental building block;
to shape, to mold, to serve.
A compound element of intelligence,
strength, and nerve.

It has the properties of being
strong and resolute.
Properties which increase with age
from an abundance in youth.

Soft Iron is the fiber from which
we weave the suit of Blue.
This diet, when in crisis, makes
a man wear hero's shoes.

Soft Iron is the steady strength
and the guiding hand
Of our street warriors who
protect this native land.

Most turbulent is the strife unheard
and the enemy unseen,
Most dangerous are the battles
where the enemy must first be screened.

Listening to the Corn

Such warriors must be wise and just
and observe a selfless creed.
They sacrifice their safety
to protect all from criminal deeds.

This mission they graciously accept,
thanks and praise they receive with demure.
Impossible tasks they shoulder bravely
and smile, because that's what soft iron is for.

Gerard A. Geiger   May 30, 2000

Gerard A. Geiger

On Writing Poetry

I am trying to figure out what and why I want to write today.
Something is troubling me…bubbling to the surface.
I started thinking about it yesterday.

Some common thread had presented itself to me…
It is elusive…like trying to grasp a droplet of mercury.
An idea is there, however I know it.

I must wait until the communication lines are open
to receive this latest insight or gift.
Where these ideas or intuitions come from is a mystery.

I don't know whether they are bursts of light, explosions of
thought or the congealed remains of subconscious magma
distilled after years of dripping, collecting, pouring, gurgling,
and meandering their way through to consciousness.

I only report these as they occur, though occasionally I can
retrieve portions by dipping a conscious ladle into the vat of my
data bank and lift the skin of this warmed milk.

Of one thing I am certain, the volume of the vat is incalculable.

Gerard A. Geiger   26 October 2000

Effects

Why write?

Who am I to write?
Who am I to share?
Who am I to feel?

I am I.

There surely is no other…I
But, there may be you…
Surely, there is a you…

If, this you

knows of Me…
then we have created a change.
The sum of the changes

is the effect of our Poetry.

Gerard A. Geiger   6 Nov 2000

Gerard A. Geiger

Autumnal Protest

A flock of dried oak leaves
with ruffled edges
shuffle in the breeze,
jockeying for position
before each new gust of wind.

Then spring forth
mounting the calm and barren sky
peppering the placid canvas
with silhouettes, the silent
signatures of their former lush green selves.

The activity reminiscent
of their pliant days,
when sap filled their veins
and little girls
peeled them away from their stems.

Placed them between
their upheld thumbs
and blew whistles to the boys
they dared to play against
when hiding and seeking.

Now these leaves
hurtle before the wind
confused and jumbled,
hesitant in their motion,
bending and breaking.

Listening to the Corn

Rousted from their beds
and propelled forth,
rushed through their agony
of feebleness
to embrace

The creased and rumpled
bed of mulch;
the last place
of melded firmament
for their final nurturing repose.

Gerard A. Geiger   7 November 2000

Gerard A. Geiger

Mind Traveler

What thought is this,
peeking over the horizon?
A dull light obscured
by rolling wisps of fog.
What words do I use
as stepping stones
to bridge this gap?

A Mind Traveler, not limited
to space, time, and physical laws;
I build my case
one word at a time,
capturing the essence
of thought or emotion
and bring it to light.

My range is from
the infinitesimal
to the infinite.
I have no boundaries.
This is at once
exhilarating and
frightening.

Exhilarating for the chase
and chance
of discovery.
Frightening for the possibility
of losing my way,

Listening to the Corn

without a string
to follow for finding my way back.

Gerard A. Geiger   November 17, 2000

Closure

Huddled on the windswept walk,
a collection over time;
stretching the thin plastic barrier,
edges protruding through the membrane.

An amniotic sack of gifts,
notes and special trinkets;
emotional landmarks that pointed
to a growing relationship.

Shivering under the frosted dew,
sharing the company of past pleasures;
aimlessly speculating in the comforting
cocoon of blissful mystery and wonder.

Lifted from its naked spot
by a stranger with sticky soiled gloves
and thrown onto the threshing bed
for the fresh cut stew of decay.

There to await, under subdued gasps,
as the hydraulic arms compress
the plunger of the compactor
forcing all to face their inglorious end.

Gerard A. Geiger   28 November 2000

Chance of Love

I have never met you before.
Did not recognize your face.
Yet there is something familiar
in your aspect and your grace.

What kindred spirit must you be?
To what pheromone spell have I succumbed?
Why with just a glance am I beguiled?
When to all else I am benumbed.

How much of love is left to chance?
What conscious decisions have we made?
With the bread of love already baked,
we spread just the marmalade.

Gerard A. Geiger   17 December 2000

Gerard A. Geiger

Winter Woods

Stripped, naked,
shivering in the wind
Cracked and corrugated
platelets of bark
offer a crusty
loosely calculated warmth.

Tentacles reaching
into the sky
blindly searching
for nourishment,
a reverse root system
fanning outward;

each appendage
carrying the crooked gait
of its history in the gnarled,
stunted, redirected
and emergent ascendancy
of limbs.

With great and solemn effort
the grey ghost-like spires
pierce the sky,
offering themselves as barnacled
reeds to produce the whispers and moans
of subconcious sleep.

While deep within
cells slowly diffuse

Listening to the Corn

bringing the artesian
springs to the hungry mouths of buds
yearning for the warmth of the light
to set them free.

Gerard A. Geiger   December 22, 2000

Gerard A. Geiger

Honour

The official charge had been given.
Over the fields the men were driven.
Fragments of metal, hurled through air,
smote them down and buried them there.

A red stream flowed across the plain.
Upon its banks the battle waned.
Discharging muskets, so often repeated,
barked with no mercy at the defeated.

At dusk the somber scene lay still.
The night cast down its dark death chill.
No warmth was found on that field.
The dead no longer push or yield.

Outlined by the moon a soldier stood
on a hill overlooking the field of blood.
The stars of night were gleaming brightly.
Those on his shoulders were tarnished slightly.

Shaking his head, with his arms opened wide,
trying to embrace those who had died.
Brave soldiers all, he had commanded;
now lay still with justice demanded.

Muttering a curse and heaving a sigh,
he grasped the pistol at his side.

Listening to the Corn

Placing the muzzle against his head,
he repented; then left to join the dead.

Gerard A. Geiger   Dec 21, 1976

Gerard A. Geiger

View of a Field in February

A large rectangular sheet of crumpled parchment,
bleached white, fitted perfectly
between two long and low piles of rock borders.

The shaded surface formed and fit over irregularities,
a mosaic of stark white and pale grays stretched thin
in the weak morning light.

Shaggy tufts of rough grass
shake their unruly honeyheads through, intermittently
and quietly asserting their independence.

Tracks of a solitary animal diagonally traverse the placid surface,
perforating the unbroken expanse of purity
with the privileged marks of its existence.

A subdued hue of blue-gray fog and overcast sky
slowly swells with the heat of
the hidden sun, then expands and cracks,

spilling searing wands of light
onto ice crystals; releasing them from
their suspended animation.

    Gerard A. Geiger   26 February 2001

Listening to the Corn

Generation of a Stream

Droplets formed and rolled together,
uniting at the lowest levels;
building strength.
Quietly moving on, while
merging with other groups of similar
masses traveling in the same direction.
Ever growing,

becoming an undulating surface
of countless minor peaks.
Refracting light in angles and arcs,
creating a shimmering scaled
whole; moving and gurgling its
frothy way over a sloping
mountain hillside.

Catching itself when
meeting an obstacle,
gathering force from superior numbers;
welling up, overflowing and cascading down.
Reconnoitering at the base
in a pool carved by the diligence
and might of its ancestors.

Revolving up to
break the surface
with the capture and release
of a quick bubble;
exclaiming its delight at this brief

chance to proclaim its rights to
freedom and change.

Without hesitating, meshing with
Its fellows as they unceasingly
explore the open terrain,
searching low spots to fill
and thus conquer;
in their quest to
engulf all in their path.

Stopping at nothing to overcome
by will of their interconnectedness,
acting as a single organism.
Seeking universal fulfillment
and ending their lifetime mission
by joining together to celebrate
in the vast salted pool of their brotherhood.

Wallowing there for
perhaps an eternity,
circulating to the depths and surface,
as a chosen few slowly evaporate,
while the remainder wonder at
their disappearance,
and rumor those few

Listening to the Corn

must make the
journey again.

Gerard A. Geiger   March 6, 2001

Heron

Dusty blue gray palette
fading into white.
Lean, long, and angular.
Moving with a deliberate slow pace.
Neck arched backwards cradling
the stiletto beak.

Stepping furtively through
shallows keenly aware of
all movements within its sphere.
Lifts an elbow jointed leg,
Slowly nods its head and labors an ungainly way
along the fringe of marsh.

Suddenly,
without a telling effort,
releases its rapier beak.
Swiftly and silently skewers
unsuspecting prey; a chub, crawfish,
or small rodent.

Pauses proudly,
securing its hold of life and death.
Unfolds the matted expanse of wings,
thunders mightily into
the sky through
vapor laden air.

A master hunter,
feared and unforgiving,

Listening to the Corn

an array of one gliding home
with food;
providing nourishment
for his growing chicks.

Gerard A. Geiger   August 6, 2001

Gerard A. Geiger

I Dream of Dancing in the Streets

It is 2001.
Vietnam has long been over.
55,000 American Soldiers died in eleven years.
There are no more Protests in the Street.
"Hell no. We won't go!"
is the faded battle cry of those who were to save humanity
or themselves.

Where did all this love of humanity go?
The real war of the modern and mechanized world
plays out in the drama of senseless killing
and dismemberment on our American highways.
40,000 to 50,000 Americans are killed each year.
Every year. Even the years before
and after Vietnam.

In 10 years, 400 to 500,000 people die, and so on.
We all can do the math!
Where is the cry of protest?
What family has not been touched
by this slaughter?
Driving to work is more dangerous
than serving in the Military during a war…In a war zone!

Where are the protestors?
Is everyone so enamored
of the automobile
that we are willing to sacrifice
the lives and health of our friends and relatives

Listening to the Corn

to this economic beast?
Yes, economic beast!

Automobiles are the number one
product of America...Yes, the mechanical horse.
Almost every family has at least two
in their front or back yard.
Next to the home mortgage, they
constitute the single largest
expense of a household budget.

The expenses seemingly never end:
Purchase price; tax; registration; maintenance;
Gas; oil; insurance; storage;
Medical expenses; legal expenses;
Court costs; accident costs; death
Or perhaps dismemberment
Or disfigurement.

But look at the jobs the automobile industry creates:
GM, Chevrolet, Ford, Chrysler, Honda,
Hyundai, Nissan, Toyota, Mitsubishi,
Yamaha, Ferrari, Volvo,
Volkswagen, etc.
Parts manufacturers; oil producers
And refineries (Exxon, Mobil, Texaco, etc.).

Surely let's not forget the land development
and improvement efforts providing
hundreds of thousands of miles of paved roads.
The aggregate square miles of parking lots and
engineering masterpieces of bridges, and elevated parking
garages.

The total volume of steel, concrete, cement and asphalt
required to build and maintain the infrastructure to support
this transportation system.

This has become a way of life!
One which started out serving us, but now
one which we serve with our dead, maimed and crippled
children, family, lovers, and friends.
Who or what is so important that they, or it,
deserves this great offering of our collective wealth
and humanity?

The complacent people
we seem to have become,
may say…"oh, we can't change all of that!!!"
Yet more children and family members will die tomorrow.
"Besides, I wear my seatbelt and have an airbag".
Still, most people would not float over Niagara Falls in a padded
barrel so equipped.

Silly? Yes, but a transportation system for the masses
Should be as safe as its precious cargo needs to ensure
Safe passage for the least physically and mentally capable
among us.
THE DRUNK DRIVER IS NOT THE PROBLEM.
A truly safe transportation system should be able to be used
by Drunks, cripples, the blind, epileptics, the old, infants,
and animals, with an equal degree of safety for life and limb.

We are intelligent enough to create such a system.
We know we are.
As an example, a new substitute
Could be an underground system of transcontinental subways

Listening to the Corn

Running on superconductive electricity with magnetic
Charges for the cars which REPEL and prevent accidents…
The idea is…there are other methods which are
Less costly in lives and fortunes
in the long run.

Let's really protect our children…
Let's get them there in one piece for peace…
Let the PROTESTS begin!!!
Eventually, maybe, it will be safe enough to
Dance in the Streets.

Gerard A. Geiger   August 13, 2001

Gerard A. Geiger

Barefoot

Walking on dew covered planks
worn and soft
with a trace of moss.
Padding to the deck entrance
testing grass temperature and condensation
with a naked white soled foot.

Pushing off,
immersing ten toes in the pliable soft
cool wet strands
which scatter between each toe
embracing the foot and ankle
in a light hold of natural affection.

Bearing down
pressing the subtle sponge
of sod,
feeling earth below absorb
and return the transfer
of body temperature.

Then to the cool and barren
flagstone,
haughty and impenetrable,
as with measured step
I retrieve my morning paper
from the walk.

Gerard A. Geiger   August 14, 2001

Sideshow

Eight legs
strong and agile
centered in a net

feeling every
nuance of activity
affecting the strands,

held together
by cross-strings
at regular intervals,

alert poised
and ready for attack
waiting for a hapless wanderer.

A cross-string bends
A seventh leg slightly trembles
eight legs spring to action.

The whiskered ball hurtles
down the net and wraps
eight armlegs around

A detained confused
spectator; deftly spinning
and winding with gossamer thread.

With prey secure
armlegs release
and hunter drops

Gerard A. Geiger

from the silken screen,
swings back on its tether
and victoriously climbs hand over hand

in front of the porch light
as unwitting fans
parade and dance, destined to feed more than ego.

Gerard A. Geiger   August 18, 2001

Note: Watching with my son, Shawn, through the back porch doorway.

Listening to the Corn

An overcast noon in September,
I grab my cap and staff,
set out on a country walk.

The crowned road winds
through a wooded gully, bordering
fields atop cultivated hills.

Steadily I climb,
approaching a placid
crowd of corn;

intersected by roadway,
spilling over borders
populating the hilltop.

Each stalk,
tarnished green to brown,
shoulder to shoulder; rustling.

Talking in old
and familiar tones
through the eddy of a light breeze.

Sharing secrets
of the wind and rain
as only corn stalks know.

A charcoal cloud
meanders overhead pushing
a retinue of blustery winds.

Gerard A. Geiger

Stalks shiver and shake
in animated conversation
rolling in a wave of emotion.

Droplets of rain
punctuate the speculation,
wetting the dust of their prime.

Charcoal to light gray,
wind and rain subside;
releasing a collective sigh,

as parched husks
sip a last toast
among aged veterans,

before the cold arrives.

Gerard A. Geiger September 25, 2001

Mill Pond Falls

Seated in late afternoon
on the riverbank
between the bridge
and dam of the old Mill:

Four stories of red clapboard sided
drapery cloaking a wood beam
and dowel superstructure, a marvel
of the simple machine age.

Enthroned on the curved bank,
served by its own channel and water wheel,
as the antiquated mechanism
plods its weary way; unable to stop time.

Next to the channel is the dam,
an expanse of thirty yards,
having a drop of six feet.
Creating a mill pond with a three inch overflow.

Thirty yards of water, three inches deep,
spilling over the dam; falling six feet;
always moving; yet always there and always new;
always creating the same ceaseless patterns.

Upriver the surface of the stream is animated
with peaks and drifts, dappled with currents
until it merges with the deeper Mill pond.
Then it melds into the calm shallow basin,

Gerard A. Geiger

Smooth surfaced with gentle ripples
and gossamer knitted crazy quilts of
leaves, bark and autumn dust flowing
slowly and solidly towards the precipice.

There to break into striated strands
creating smooth, unbroken, six foot columns
from the top surface to the frothy bottom;
shaded in broad bands of white, gray, and white again.

Thirty yards wide and six feet high,
a solid wall of white ribbon candy
permanent in its look and motion,
yet scored with the intermittent

bat-winged shading of a leaf or branch
as it hurtles over the falls, coerced
to mesh with the bottom foam;
propelled on its last hurrah

before committing to begin again.

    Gerard A. Geiger   September 29, 2001

Old Red Mill, Clinton, N.J.

Gerard A. Geiger

Oak in the Woods

Walking a narrow country roadway
between hills covered with trees.
Below the road grade
a rainfall watershed
creek slithers placidly.

I review the forestation:
shagbark hickory, ash, maple and tulip poplar
dominate, with an occasional
sentient oracle of pin oak
proudly braced by surface rock;
holding on and probing deeper through
the slim contours of glacial terrain.

Around a curve an ancient specimen of oak
presents its array, four foot in diameter,
rising to a weathered tattered fork, fifty foot high.
At the base are fallen remains
of its once proud plumage.
Decaying and scattered limbs slowly
sinking into the substrate.

Trunk, gnarled and barren,
exposing the flesh colored
undercoat of hardwood, reserved
only for the most intimate of woodland
partners. Now exposed along the entire length
as the main shaft twists backward,

Listening to the Corn

arched and posed provocatively with tattered stubs of limbs;
au naturale, Venus de Milo.

Under its tender armpit are the
chiseled entrances to four
woodland apartments.
Inhabited presently by tiny clawed creatures
evidenced by the furry veneer of their
delicately clawed surfaces, which fade
into the black, deep and secret interior.

I am overcome with the utility of nature.
Witnessing this strong and resilient oak
brought slowly to the full
embrace of its surroundings.
As it melds, so we all shall meld.
May we all age so gracefully and
graciously as we weather the
ravages of time and our own explorations.

Gerard A. Geiger   January 9, 2002

Gerard A. Geiger

Structure

I like winter landscapes
revealed by
defrocked forests.

I like the patterns of
random rock formations
along hillsides.

I like peeking into
the crevices
of split glacial rock

and following the contours
of ground, dipping into every
little stream and creek.

I enjoy following the land
and singling out
the largest trees.

Wondering why these
avoided the
woodcutters' saws.

Then I make a mental landscape
how it must have looked
150 years ago.

I remove every tree smaller than two feet
in diameter and concentrate on the lay
of the land without trees or underbrush.

Listening to the Corn

Bare and barren is the result
with startling formations,
such as rock walls built by long dead farmers,

which separate abandoned fields;
wholly hidden, obscured and unobserved
during spring and summer.

I reintroduce myself to my favorite places
and visit them searchingly during these
cold and colorless days.

I find I appreciate my surroundings
a little better during
the flush and shadow of summer,

now that I am intimate with the
cold gray and granite
structure underneath.

Gerard A. Geiger   January 9, 2002

Gerard A. Geiger

Why does a Poet write?

A Poet writes because he needs to.
Not merely because he wants to.
Simply, he has to.
He is driven to make his ideas known.
Not to anyone in particular, but to all at large.

A poet is not a megalomaniac…
or an egomaniac,
but he may indeed be some other
kind of maniac.
He probably really does not know, just like the rest of us.

He is driven by the urge to exert his authority of life
by exclaiming simply, quietly and eloquently
that he exists. That he saw, he felt,
he breathed, he thought,
he was here…

That at one time or another
during his brief reign
over his own body,
on earth, he had something to say
and he said it…

not for monetary gain or personal gain,
but to add his ingredient
into the primordial mental soup of experience
left to simmer in the thought cauldron
of the archives of mankind…

Listening to the Corn

To add his one little tidbit
of mental flavor
for analysis, inclusion
or rejection by
those who will follow…

To a poet, to do less than this, is not to have lived at all.

Gerard A. Geiger   January 11, 2002

Gerard A. Geiger

Bison
(Ode to the American Buffalo)

A beast of burden it is not.
No yoke adorns its crown.
Majestic, and stoic of stature;
master of the open ground.

Lungs heave as bellows,
sending snorts of pleasure and pain
from the massive bearded head
on a thickly carpeted mane.

Forelegs draped with sinews,
to push or pull or run,
carrying the mighty torso
over plains from sun to sun.

Such nobles led great herds,
of millions were their number;
meant to last for time to come,
but not immune to plunder.

For what was ripe in beauty
and lordly in its bearing,
became not a source of food,
but rich robes for the wearing.

Quickly herds were slaughtered.
The meat rotted in the sun.
Few beasts were left remaining
when all was said and done.

Listening to the Corn

What is left is the legacy
of the beast, strong and proud;
for it survived the fashion
and truth now is its shroud.

Gerard A. Geiger   April 2, 1986

Gerard A. Geiger

Thaw

Hiking a steep country roadway
on a balmy day in February.
The temperature hit 52 degrees,
a new record high.

Walking briskly,
deeply inhaling fresh
country air mingled with
a musty scent of furrowed fields.

Gazing at stubble stalks
of harvested corn surrounded
by Holstein patches
of melting snow.

Feeling the cracked
awakening of sheltered pores,
beads of sweat oozing under
a light cover of clothes.

Ascending a hilltop
as a summit breeze fans
each wetted orifice,
cooling tender surfaces

under arms and thighs
and probing around temples,
neck and sides;
gently massaging and awakening

Listening to the Corn

dormant follicles of hair
singularly cooled by the wind,
caressing and whispering
promises of an early spring.

Gerard A. Geiger   February 2002

Gerard A. Geiger

Chat with Dr. Hereford

Approaching a sheltered hillside,
slightly wooded with creek;
encircled with a single row
of wire supporting ceramic marshmallows.

In the center stands Dr. Hereford,
solid and pensive
chewing wistfully
on a single wand of straw.

"Good morning Dr! I see you're
in the lower pasture this week!" I exclaim
good naturedly. He nods, grunts, and
laboriously moves closer to a split hay bale.

Feeling slightly rebuffed, I explain
"I know I'm early for my appointment,
but why not make good use of this encounter?"
Dr. Hereford shrugs thick shoulders.

He knows these chats
are at the quarter hour rate,
and my requirement for thrift
subconsciously directs me

towards these seemingly
coincidental meetings

Listening to the Corn

at chance intersections
to obtain his solemn and reflective advice.

He moves half a step away
lowers his head and slyly
looks sideways to ensure I'm
still patiently waiting my turn.

"Meeeoouugh!" He states emphatically.
I apologize for imposing
on his good graces without
a scheduled appointment.

"Meeeoouugh!" He states again
with finality as he lifts his head
in response to a distant bell.
He turns with dignity and trots off.

I am left alone, to solve
my problems on my own time
and in my own way,
just as Dr. Hereford suggests.

Gerard A. Geiger   June 11, 2002

Gerard A. Geiger

The Grain Field

Standing on the access road
overgrown with grasses,
rutted from deep lugged
tread of farm equipment.

Looking over the expanse
of the grain field,
waist high and still growing.
Each strand visible, unique,

all perfect clones
of uniform thickness and height.
Their tips ending in clusters
of rye kernels.

Altogether appearing as
a substantial permanent whole,
yet upon inspection
each strand moves slightly.

Sometimes in unison
with its brothers and at
other times dancing to
a forward or backward eddy.

Yet never totally still…
Occasionally the parapet

Listening to the Corn

of rest for a cricket, but
always with crown held high

expectantly waiting,
uniformly shouldering
the shared burdens of
heat, wind and rain…

Stalwart and sincere
murmuring in collective whispers
and sighs…content to be…
without demands from tomorrow.

Save a little light
and a dram of rain.

Gerard A. Geiger   June 24, 2002

Gerard A. Geiger

Disinherited

Captured through guile and trickery
forced to assemble en masse
shackled stranger to stranger
transported to foreign climes.

Deprived of personal mobility
sharing fetid air
no subsistence rationed
to augment body fat.

Release of bowels
and regurgitation
in human slop
infested holds.

Baking and bobbing,
shackled and sickly;
forgotten, forlorn, deprived,
unwashed and uncared for.

Beaten, cowed,
battered and broken;
assaulted, raped
and spit upon.

Sold as property,
distressed, disheveled
and dispirited; naked
with all orifices probed.

Listening to the Corn

Herded in pens,
whipped to work.
Herded to sleep,
whipped to work.
Forced to mate,
whipped to work.
Forced to procreate,
whipped to work.
Children produced and violated,
whipped to work.
Generation after generation violated,
whipped to work

…Until reluctantly released to death.

Tormented and tortured
generations, through family lines,
whipped to work…with
no profit from their labors

From corporations which trace profits
through generations of incorporations.
Profits which still exist today…spent and
hoarded by great great grandsons of slavers.

While descendants, no longer
shackled and appearing free,
are economic casualties
of forced disinheritance…

Denial of birthright and succession are
economic consequences of slavery.

Gerard A. Geiger

I realize as I write this poem on a 19th century
desk handed down from my Ancestors.

Gerard A. Geiger   July 1, 2002

Note: written for the U.S. 4th of July 2002, Independence Day.
Apologetically dedicated to descendants and victims
of slavery and economically deprived aboriginal populations
throughout the world.

Hunting

In a clearing
on an overgrown field
next to a crawling river,

I step firmly
on the shoulder
of the shovel blade.

The iron face slices
through moist layers
of leaves and loam.

I lift and turn
each spoonful exposing
a pile in reverse chronology.

Sediment and stone
appear on the mound
of newly turned earth.

A wedge shaped
stone little smaller than
a brick is exposed.

I feel its comfortable
shape in my hand,
smooth, soft and worn;

with noticeable marks
of wear on the ends,
where it was used for crushing.

Gerard A. Geiger

The center is ground
with a channel
to attach a handle,

Or use as a
handhold for
Stone Age convenience.

Dimly,
I feel the being
who fashioned

this primitive tool.
His hybrid animalism
peeking through the ages,

captured in the
contours of utility
held in my dirty hand.

Gerard A. Geiger   July 7, 2002
Note: Thoughts on finding an Indian artifact on my property.

Mother Corn

Cylindrical rows of
golden cobblestones
nestled in receiving
blankets of husks.

Cradled and favored one
to a mother,
marching single file
in columns of tasseled stalks.

The annual graduating
class of maidens
with product for the world
to nourish the masses.

Cultivated by each
doting parent and
wrapped in whorled leaves
of protection,

each nurtures
her progeny
and dutifully sends
every cultivated charge

off with missionary
zeal to feed

Gerard A. Geiger

the humble rabble,
or to store its life force

ruminating in silos to
await the gnashing
jaws of life
to which it owes its fealty.

Providing food for the present,
seeds for the ages,
life for the future,
ensuring the cycle continues.

…Endlessly giving.

Gerard A. Geiger   July 9, 2002

Social Physics

Two ancient cultures,
equally strong in their beliefs,
meeting on the shores
of virgin islands.

One searching for
riches and empowerment,
the other content
to be.

One using technical
innovation to subjugate
and enslave...
forcing its will.

The other accepting change with
cooperation, feeding,
teaching, and assisting
new friends to share.

One avaricious without
limits to cruelty and greed.
The other unlimited in ability to
compromise, nurture and coexist.

Two separate ancient cultures:
One rapacious, domineering, cruel

Gerard A. Geiger

with boundless greed, meeting
one without industry or pestilence,

trying to cooperate to achieve
homeostasis with its new environmental
neighbors. Not understanding
that annihilation results

when matter and antimatter meet.

Gerard A. Geiger   July 15, 2002

Note: Thoughts on European discovery of America

Interlude

Summer is a state of being
accompanied by warm weather.

Rev up the metabolism
sweat out starchy pores.

Feel a pulse throb in the ears,
deeply inhale tepid damp air.

Cool down in sweat soaked t-shirt
feel soft vegetation on naked thighs.

Release feet from stifled bondage
allow soft pale skin to tan.

Rediscover sensitive folds of skin
massaged by water and air.

Wonder at the great expanse of earth
and the minor portion we experience.

Know we belong unfettered
splashing in puddles and oozing through mud,

Gerard A. Geiger

walk in rain and wind
step with wet sneakers.

In awe of the height and width of trees
surrounded by lush foliage.

Find a clearing in which to stand
through passing gusts of wind.

Meld with surroundings
…as just another blade of grass.

Gerard A. Geiger July 18, 2002

Sentinel

The clarions had sounded,
reverberating through the land.
The call was made to muster
for every able-bodied man.

From the hills and valleys,
from each hamlet and town,
poured the country's champions;
young, still dressed in down.

All their adolescent dreams,
their wishes, loves and more…
were offered with their honor
at the altar of war.

They accepted the mantle,
the yoke of the free,
the obligation to preserve
their country's liberty.

For this they fought the battles.
Some were wounded. Some died.
Each life was forever altered
by their refusal to hide.

To those silent sentinels,
the guardians of the night,
who insured our peaceful homes
and sheltered our children from fright.

Gerard A. Geiger

We give our thanks and praise
for the sacrifice they bore,
and pledge always to remember
their gift of service in war.

Gerard A. Geiger   March 23, 1996

Autumn Wind

Welcome back my blustery friend.
I missed your gentle summer prodding
during the humid stillborn days of August.

It is good to smell the northern freshness
surrounding your cool
and quickening bellows.

There is a trace of age,
of overuse and staleness,
in your autumn touch.

I trust it is the withering
of summer that
casts this mellow scent to your breath.

I breathe deeply of all your travels.
I can taste the newly mowed fields
and roll the dust of harvest on my tongue.

I fill my lungs with
bales of your wanderings
and warmly welcome home my freshly traveled friend.

Gerard A. Geiger   13 September 2002

Gerard A. Geiger

Raptor

Oh gently gliding instrument,
effortlessly rising,
floating on
billowing pillows of air.

Surveying the countryside
with a jewelers eye
for small details
and fleet movements.

Streamlined silhouette,
circling in ever growing arcs,
tracing the needlework connecting
fields and newly turned earth.

Searching, seeking, with
penetrating vision,
uncovering the subterfuge
of camouflage and natural selection.

Finding the target,
homing in with sharpened senses,
diving with a single thought
while clenching its talons.

Pulling up and grasping
in a final instant,
as it lightly touches earth
and rises with its quarry.

Listening to the Corn

Now to feed upon its catch,
perhaps share with its family,
then return to the hunt
efficient, sleek and elegant,

the consummate Survivor.

Gerard A. Geiger   September 13, 2002

Gerard A. Geiger

Birch 101

I step along an old logging trail,
round a corner, and am confronted by
a family of Birches.

The oldest, twelve inches in diameter
with a height of forty feet,
wrapped in wafer thin white papyrus.

Inscribed all along the trunk
at regular intervals with black
spots and dashes,

the cryptic chronology
of its existence
patiently etched in its frayed coat.

Crowded among younger birches
where all note, read and decipher
when bowed with winter snow,

as they confer on family matters
in the coded secrecy
of birch to birch education.

    Gerard A. Geiger   September 15, 2002

Flutterspeed

On a hilltop
Overlooking harvested fields
A platoon of telephone
poles stagger their

march over the crest
and down the other side.
Attached to the cross piece
are two wires.

On the wires roost
a small flock of sparrows
appearing as discs
on a simple abacus.

Without warning
the sparrows lift off
in consecutive order from the left
like a delicate ribbon

Caught in a gust of
wind flattening out as it twists,
then thickening as it
turns with minimum sound

of chirping, just the
feather duster ruffle of their
plumage as they fan their hurried
way through improvised choreography.

Gerard A. Geiger

The ruffling wanes and
increases with the difficulty
of maneuver, as predictable
as the crescendo at a race track.

As the swarm circles
back around me, I
am immersed in their vortex
and swear such precision

could never be controlled
with strings.

Gerard A. Geiger September 15, 2002

October at Oxford Lake

An armada of Canada geese
plow over a string of
caution colored red floats,

daring to explore the
unknown placid regions
of an unmarked surface.

In the background plush
piles of carpeted forest
loom as a natural safety barrier

protecting and preserving
the serenity of a season
past its prime...

where only the memories
of children gleefully shrieking
and busily splashing

are distantly felt
rather than heard
as the tufted backdrop

changes its mottled
color to mimic the garish
hues of yellow and red,

Gerard A. Geiger

colors which caution
of winters steady climb
and summers all too quick

fall from grace

Gerard A. Geiger   October 22, 2002

Herald of Winter

Stopping to rest
beside a telephone pole
on a windblown hill.

Listening to the
whistle of wind
through split wires, while overhead

gray bottomed clippers,
with cotton candy sheets,
sail from north to east;

a troposphere
flotilla moving towards
its winter home.

No guiding beacon
to direct the motions
of these ghost ships,

just the rustle applause
of wind whipping through
the tree line,

sole spectators between fields,
who intercept and comment
on each change of wind direction

and telegraph its future destination
to expectant and waiting hosts
as a whistle between wires;

Gerard A. Geiger

the party line
on which I eavesdrop
this November afternoon.

Gerard A. Geiger   November 20, 2002

Without Love

A life without love
is a barren field.
A place of rocks
and dirt with
little vegetation,

minimal growth
establishing minor
root systems,
barely able to
withstand erosion

from wind and rain.
Suffering alone the indignities
of heat, cold and drought.
Hanging on through
passing seasons

with no yardstick
to measure personal growth.
One viewpoint, one life,
without complication
and without worth.

A futile effort
to avoid humility
without passing on the
benefit of experience.
Making no attempt

Gerard A. Geiger

to create something better
in this world.

Gerard A. Geiger   Nov 23 2002

Imponderable

A pane of glass,
the final filter
for a light perhaps
billions of years old.

Refracted in my retina
and registering
in my consciousness
as a tiny point

between me and infinity.
A simple concept, really,
if it actually is just a
point of light.

But a light quite
bright showing
early evening
through the earth atmosphere

could easily
signify a distant galaxy,
which appears over
an immeasurably great distance

as a single point of
light from my perspective.
This same source of light has probably
been observed through

Gerard A. Geiger

infinite pairs of eyes
over the billions of years
of its existence…and is the closest
quality this insignificant human

will ever know
of the concept of a GOD.
…All else is shadow,
superstition, and innuendo.

Gerard A. Geiger   Nov 23, 2002

Dissonance

I hate you…

I study how you hold your head,

how you nod when you greet friends.

I see your quizzical smile displaying

a sliver of straight white teeth

behind full lips, which are quick to

pucker in consternation, amazement or

mock sincerity,

followed by a disarming throaty

laugh which trails off into

a girlish giggle.

A knowing nod and a flip of a

wave with a delicate long-fingered

hand airily held high,

polished nails of shimmering rubies

swirling in the doorway as you lightly

turn, swish your skirt, and exit

to the great parking lot beyond…

Gerard A. Geiger

I would follow…but then…

I hate you.

Gerard A. Geiger			Nov 29, 2002

Germination

Trees, crisp with
coats of velvet frost.
Fog creeps into every niche.
Caw of crow
resonates through
vapor laden
mist.

Breath billows
with every labored step.
Rust squealing
rollers
exclaim their surprise
as the mammoth
plank door
slices its way open,

allowing a wedge
of sunlight
to penetrate the
cavern,
spilling over machines,
illuminating stained wood floors;
raising embedded smells
of hay, gas, oil and manure.

I stretch,
deeply breathe
the musty scent

Gerard A. Geiger

of the awakening day.
From this
dusty embryo
germinate thoughts and actions
that feed the world.

Gerard A. Geiger   Nov 30, 2002

Spring House

Down the footpath
we scuffed and clambered

on worn hard soil
between glacial rock

interspersed with tufts of
long slender grass,

wild onions and ferns.

At the bottom stood
the spring house,

a sturdy wooden
structure encasing the

small pool of water,

which bubbled up and
overflowed through a sluice channel

exiting at the bottom of the
southernmost wall.

It was here
we told confidences

embraced and explored
sheltered and secure

Gerard A. Geiger

enveloped in our own
newly discovered mystery.

Gerard A. Geiger   December 9, 2002

Country Graveyard

A three foot high
fieldstone wall
two foot deep
in the center of
a field.

Crumbling in places
where the elements
have breached
the simple design,

enclosing an area
twenty foot square
overgrown with sumac
and riddled with holes;

abandoned marmot
channels of
kicked up debris,
a flow of dirt and shale

in front of two
gravestones
on opposite sides
of the enclosure.

Henry Miller reads one
Born 1787, died 183 something.

Gerard A. Geiger

Sarah Mowder reads the other
19 years 10 months 27 days
...faded remainder.

How precious those days
must have been for one to
live and die so young.

Was she wife and Mother?
What dreams did she dream?
Is the broken smaller gravestone
Her only attempt at immortality?

Or is it all for this poem
of unanswered thoughts and
ripe beginnings
echoing through the worm holes
of time?

Gerard A. Geiger   December 10 2002

Rat Jack

Rat Jack was royalty
among the Hoboes,
a fierce competitor for food.
No hunting animal was safe
with its catch
as long as RJ was near.

It was rumored he got his name from
following rats to find their nests.
Then he would raid their shaggy
beds and steal their newborns
for Mulligan stew.
He claimed there was no cleaner game
than newborn rats in stew.

When asked why he liked rats
so much, he would say
"everybody thinks I'm crazy for huntin and cookin rats,
but there's never a shortage of em!"
"And anyways, they ain't as pretty as a
squirrel…but, a squirrel ain't nothin more'n a tree rat
with a bushy tail!"

"When it comes to starvin"…he'd always say
"I'd Rat-her live!"

…and laugh as he skulked away.

Gerard A. Geiger   12 December 2002

Gerard A. Geiger

Economics of the Street

Ninety seven dollars
in the right denominations
can fill a wallet,

can overflow to excess,
can lead to bouts
of profligate spending,

can be used to entertain
oneself and others
at a moments notice,

can buy a dinner,
a tank of gas;
rent a bed and pillow

with just enough
left over to grab
a bite to warm the morning fog.

Ninety seven dollars,
constituent parts of
a broken "C" note,

without the haughty
austere unapproachable majesty
of a crisp Franklin, demanding thrift.

Ninety seven dollars
comfortable and warm
filling a pocket with possibility,

Listening to the Corn

with economic power
to purchase necessities or
bask in the luxury of indulgence.

It is said people born to luxury
Are indifferent to it…
And to those who want…

A luxury never tasted
is a luxury never missed.

It has been rumored
a rich man once said,
"If you have to ask the price…you can't afford it."

I have ninety seven dollars
in my pocket today,
and rich men frequently are assholes.

Gerard A. Geiger   December 23, 2002

Gerard A. Geiger

Fool for Love

Across the room
I saw her look,
her inquiring gaze
was not mistook.

She lingered there
for just a sec,
then promptly
turned a graceful neck.

Her gaze averted,
though now withdrawn,
was still a memory
to capitalize on.

She turned back again
for another stare,
perhaps to seek
exposure there.

I was ready when
she made her move,
willing and able to show
my love.

Her eyes met mine,
it was my chance
to secure my love
without dalliance.

Listening to the Corn

I blinked one eye,
blew a kiss,
and smiled so wide
she couldn't miss.

She stood up, waved,
and gaily ran,
past my open arms
to her waiting man.

After this event
I made a rule:
When love's involved,
I'll be a fool.

Gerard A. Geiger   January 18, 2003

Gerard A. Geiger

Flip-Flop

I never cared much
for flip-flops.
Most of us know
them as thongs.

They offer little
support for
fallen arches
and barely protect the sole.

Yet, yesterday I saw
a pair in pink with
a single white daisy
attached to each strap.

In them were two
perfectly formed
thirty year old feet,
smooth, uncallused,

with pink painted
toenails, clipped
and cared for,
with a slight tan.

I only saw them
briefly, and I
can't say why
I remember…

Listening to the Corn

because I really
don't care much
for flip-flops.

Gerard A. Geiger			February 16, 2003

Gerard A. Geiger

Cold Creek and Ice

It's a cold day in February
The wind is busy
churning the frigid
heart of winter.

I walk on a slight rise
above a spring fed creek.
This is the third day
I have watched this creek
in temperatures below 20 degrees
and ice has formed.

First, along the fringe of bank
adding thickness and height
just above the surface.
Then the ice creeps inward

adding bits of width in slight layers,
slowly building a
contour line canopy
encroaching the free space
suspended over the faster water
in the middle of the creek.

This is the final hurdle,
the most difficult expanse to cover,
accomplished with the slightest
layer of ice crystals

formed of vapor suspended
above the channel which adheres

Listening to the Corn

to the thicker walls and finally
merges to form the slightest
translucent ice bubble which fully covers
the final sliver of creek.

If it thaws tomorrow, this engineering
marvel will melt and be gone.
If the cold continues, it will thicken
and establish a winter runway

for our ground bound creatures
to traverse in search of food.

I have seen it all ways…
and like the delicate bubble
best.

    Gerard A. Geiger   February 23, 2003

Gerard A. Geiger

He is...

He is tall now,
no longer looks up
at me adoringly.

His face is shiny,
limbs are long
and bellows like a bullfrog.

He has the table
manners of a starving convict,
and an odor of a rotting pumpkin.

He grew six inches
in the past four months,
plows through clothes

and shoes like tissue.
Bumps into every fragile thing
and declares war on every chair and floor.

Girls suddenly began calling
...he suffers them with grace.
He rode several expensive bikes to death

and has parts for three more on order.
He is definitely tone deaf, but in his
heart he sings like Sinatra.

His music is too loud for
safety glass...yet he plays
it constantly while eavesdropping.

Listening to the Corn

He is behind in all his studies
and chores…and growing out
of every stitch of clothes he owns.

He is loud, dirty, smelly, obnoxious
slovenly, lazy, independent, funny,
disrespectful, and charming…

and I love him……

Because he is 14 1/2 and he is my Boy…

Gerard A. Geiger   21 February 2003

Author Biography

Listening to the Corn

Gerard Andrew Geiger, born December 27, 1953 in New Brunswick, New Jersey. Of German and Irish descent, he is the fourth of nine children from a 1950's era Catholic family. Gerard attended Catholic school through the fifth grade. At eleven years of age, in the sixth grade in 1964, Gerard began writing poetry.

After high school in 1971 he joined the Air Force, became a Security Policeman, completed a tour in South East Asia, serving in Vietnam and Thailand, and was discharged in 1975. He completed a BA in Political Science and History from Rutgers College, Rutgers University in 1977 and completed graduate school earning an MPA from Fairleigh Dickinson University in 1984.

For the past 25 years he has been employed as a Management Analyst for the Army Research Development and Engineering Center (ARDEC) in Dover, New Jersey. Gerard has lived in the pastoral country of Warren County, New Jersey for the past twenty five years. He has hiked the roads, woods and streams near his rural home and has written particularly poignant works extolling the virtue of the simple country settings and natural ambiance of northwest New Jersey country life.

When not writing poetry, Gerard walks extensively, reads history, and collects 18th and 19th century pewter and Colonial era artifacts.

"Listening to the Corn" is Gerard's second book of poetry. "This volume I believe is more personal" Gerard states, "because it deals with my most inner thoughts while I take my daily two-mile constitutional next to the farmlands bordering my home in northwest New Jersey".

0-595-27506-0